Lamborghini

Tracy Nelson Maurer

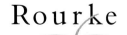

Publishing LLC
Vero Beach, Florida 32964

www.rourkepublishing.com

We recognize that some words, model names and designations, for example, mentioned herein are the property of the trademark holder. We use them for identification purposes only. This is not an official publication.

PHOTO CREDITS: All images Courtesy of Lamborghini

AUTHOR CREDITS:
The author gratefully acknowledges project assistance provided by Mark Smeyers of Lamborghini Cars at http://www.lambocars.com.

Also, the author extends appreciation to Mike Maurer, Lois M. Nelson, Margaret and Thomas, and the team at Rourke.

Editor: Robert Stengard-Olliges

Cover design by Todd Field
Page design by Nicola Stratford

Library of Congress Cataloging-in-Publication Data

Maurer, Tracy, 1965-
 Lamborghini / Tracy Nelson Maurer.
    p. cm. -- (Full throttle)
 Includes index.
 ISBN 1-60044-224-2 (hardcover)
 ISBN 978-1-60044-364-0 (paperback)
 1. Lamborghini automobile--Juvenile literature. I. Title. II. Series: Maurer, Tracy, 1965-. Full throttle.

TL215.L33M383 2006
629.222'2--dc22

                            2006017497

Printed in the USA

CG/CG

Rourke Publishing

www.rourkepublishing.com – sales@rourkepublishing.com
Post Office Box 3328, Vero Beach, FL 32964

Table of Contents

The House of the Fighting Bull

Ferruccio Lamborghini (1916-1993) grew up in the hilly farmlands of north-central Italy. Ferruccio showed an early interest in machines. He also showed no interest in farming like his father. Yet, his farm experience made him rich. After World War II, Ferruccio started building powerful farm tractors from leftover army vehicles. Soon he opened a successful tractor factory.

Ferruccio Lamborghini Milestones

- **1948** Began producing tractors at the Lamborghini Trattori factory.
- **1959** Started Lamborghini Calor Company to make oil burners, boilers, and air conditioners.
- **1963** Opened the sports car factory in Sant'Agata Bolognese near Modeno.
- **1969** Expanded into hydraulic valve manufacturing with Lamborghini Oledinamica.
- **1972** Started selling off his businesses and bought a rural estate he named "La Fiorita," where he developed a world-class golf resort and vineyard.

*Ferruccio Lamborghini was born under the zodiac sign of Taurus, or the bull. In time, he became a big fan of bullfighting. He chose a bull for his company's **marque**. It's still used today.*

marque
> the logo for an automobile manufacturer or its models

Many Lamborghini names also honored bullfighting, such as Diablo, Urraco, Bravo, and Jalpa.

The Bullfighting Connection

The Lamborghini Miura marque featured bull horns and a tail. It was the first of many Lamborghini cars connected to bullfighting, a traditional sport of Spain.

First Year	Car Name	Bullfighting Connection
1966	Miura (mee YUR ah)	The ranch in Spain known for breeding brave fighting bulls is linked to Lamborghini's friend Don Eduardo Miura.
1968	Islero (EE lair oh)	The name of the Miura bull famous for killing a popular bullfighter in 1947.
1968	Espada (es PA da)	The master bullfighter who must kill the bull. The word in Spanish means "sword."
2002	Murciélago (MUR see EH lah goh)	The name of a bull who was allowed to live because of his spirit and wits in 1879. He fathered many Miura fighting bulls.
2003	Gallardo (ga YAR doh)	One of the five main breeds of fighting bulls.

Several tales explain why wealthy Ferruccio Lamborghini built his first touring sports car. Here's the most popular story:

Lamborghini owned several fancy speedsters in 1963. He favored a locally built Ferrari except for its tricky **clutch**. Lamborghini tried to bring the problem to the car's builder, Enzo Ferrari. It seems Ferrari snubbed the tractor-maker's comments. So, Lamborghini decided to show the older Italian how to build a better touring car.

Even if it's not a true story, Lamborghini certainly succeeded in building cars that rivaled Ferrari's.

Extreme. Uncompromising. Italian. *These three key characteristics have always defined Lamborghini cars. They're known worldwide for their power, speed, reliability, quality, beauty, and high prices.*

Fast Fact

The "GT" in upscale car names usually refers to "gran turismo"—the Italian way to say "great touring."

clutch
a part of the engine's transmission used to shift gears

Lamborghini built his first 350 GTV at his tractor plant in 1963. The 350 GT models rolled out of the newly built car factory a year later.

Superstars of Supercars

Lamborghini first became the supercar to own with the stunning Miura. At the 1965 car show in Turin, Italy, Lamborghini unveiled the Miura's bare steel **chassis** with its V-12 engine mounted sideways at the car's middle. Even without a body shell, critics raved! A year later, the Miura stole the Geneva Motor Show dressed in a low-cut and curvy body shell.

- The powerful Miura lacked modern road-gripping **aerodynamics**. The front end actually lifted off the road at high speeds (the only speed for this car!).
- About 760 Miuras were built from 1966 to 1972. Since then, about half crashed or met other sad ends.
- The Miura's slinky roof stood only about 42" (107 cm) or waist high. To squeeze a normal-sized person into the car, the seats leaned uncomfortably backward.
- The Miura's lights popped up into a higher position when turned on. Otherwise, they sat too low on the car to shine on the road.

aerodynamics
engineering designs that allow air to flow easily over the body for greater speed

chassis
the frame that supports the body of a vehicle

Fast Fact

A Miura could hit 175 miles (282 km) per hour and blaze from 0 to 60 miles (97 km) per hour in 6.7 seconds.

Holy Cow!

At the Geneva Motor Show in 1971, Lamborghini followed the splashy Miura with a peek at the next superstar of supercars: the break-all-the-rules Countach (KOON tahsh). Its wide, wedge-shaped body wore grilles in angled stripes like war paint on a spaceship. The Countach wowed the world. Two years later, the Countachs finally charged out of the factory to fill overdue orders.

When he first saw the new Lamborghini design, a local Italian man exclaimed, "Countach!" It's an Italian slang way to say "Holy cow!" The name stuck.

One of the widest cars ever built, the Countach used its squat stance for nearly perfect weight balance from front to rear. This improved its handling at top speeds.

The Countach's unique, pivoting doors created a grand entrance. Small door latches tucked into the side air scoops added to the design's mystique.

Lamborghini built every Countach by hand, according to each customer's order.

Countach passengers had to shout over the massive V-12 engine G-R-O-W-L-I-N-G behind their heads. It drew on six power-boosting **carburetors**, not just one like normal cars.

carburetors
a device for mixing fuel with air for the engine to burn

The Countach snarled through four exhaust pipes. Most cars have one or two pipes.

The Countach engine blocked most of the rear view for nearly blind back-ups.

Design Detours

Money problems and design detours stalled Automobili Lamborghini more than once on its road to success. After Ferruccio Lamborghini sold the company in the 1970s, several different owners have tried to find a profitable path. The Countach kept orders coming in for nearly two decades. But the company needed more products to sell.

While Chrysler owned Lamborghini in the 1980s, design work briefly detoured to California. The American-built Lamborghini Portofino four-seater later inspired the innovative Chrysler "cab forward" Intrepid and Concorde cars.

Diablo roared into the exotic supercar world in 1990 with a snorting engine and flashy design. Two years later, Lamborghini tweaked the design and Diablo VT stamped its mark in the history books as the fastest production car in the world. It reached a top speed of 202 miles (325 km) per hour and helped confirm the company's supercar legacy.

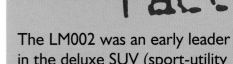

Fast Fact

The LM002 was an early leader in the deluxe SUV (sport-utility vehicle) trend.

In 1977, Lamborghini built the Cheetah as a fast, 4x4 army vehicle. No military wanted it or the later versions. Finally in 1986, Lamborghini's LM002 4x4 sparked sales with a burly V-12 engine that nailed 130 miles (210 km) per hour. Only about 300 were made.

The New Era

Lamborghini workers looked wary when yet another new owner bought Automobili Lamborghini in 1998. They had heard a lot of promises before. But the Audi branch of Volkswagen didn't try to take over. The new managers studied Lamborghini's history and drew up plans for its future. They told Lamborghini to build extreme, uncompromising, and very Italian cars again. The relieved workers set out to do just that.

Since 2001, the House of the Fighting Bull has focused on four supercars: the Murciélago and Murciélago Roadster (convertible), and the smaller, less expensive Gallardo and Gallardo Spyder (convertible).

Beautiful Beasts

The newest Lamborghini designs often steal the show at the world's major car events. Since Lamborghini revved up again in the Audi era, the Frankfurt Motor Show in Germany has heaped awards on the car company.

- **2005** Gallardo Spyder named World's Most Beautiful Sports Car
- **2004** Murciélago Roadster named World's Most Beautiful Sports Car
- **2003** Gallardo named World's Most Beautiful Sports Car
- **2001** Murciélago honored with a "Special Award"

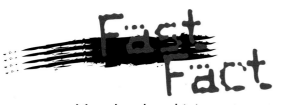

Fast Fact

Most Lamborghinis cost more than $200,000.

Lamborghinis today are not off-road 4x4s. But they do use four-wheel drive systems for better handling on curvy race tracks or icy alpine roads.

Previous Lamborghini cars drove hard, like race cars do. Today's cars feature more cushy comforts but not enough to compromise the extreme Italian sports car experience.

Lamborghini expects to sell as many as 850 new supercars to American customers each year—a huge portion of its total production. Lamborghini recently switched from the usual debut venues in Europe to exclusive preview parties and big cars shows in the United States.

The Murciélago has just one windshield wiper that clears the entire window.

A test proved that a Murciélago randomly pulled off the assembly line could crank up to 205 miles (330 km) per hour and stay there for 100 miles (161 km). It set a new world record for production cars.

The Murciélago can pop open air vents at the upper rear sides to gulp air if the engine runs hot. Otherwise, the vents stay closed for less aerodynamic drag.

Fäst Fäct

Murciélago is one of very few words to use every vowel.

On today's sports cars, the rear spoiler adds downward pressure to prevent lift-off at high speeds. The Murciélago rear spoiler actually adjusts its tilted angle for different speeds.

Batmobile?

In the 2005 movie *Batman Begins*, the Dark Knight drove a Murciélago Roadster when he wasn't cruising in his Batmobile. Funny enough, *murciélago* in Spanish means "bat."

So Alike, So Different

From their first showings, both the Murciélago and Gallardo presented features true to the Lamborghini spirit:

- Extreme speed, hovering around 200 miles (322 km) per hour
- Uncompromising performance, with nearly perfect weight distribution and all-wheel drive
- Bold Italianate design with "Privilege Programme" customizing options

So, how do these supercars measure up against each other? Check out these estimated reports:

The Gallardo's nickname is "Little Lambo."

	2006 Murciélago	2006 Gallardo
Engine	V-12 mid-mounted	V-10 mid-mounted
Horsepower	580	520
Top speed	205 mph (330 km/h)	196 mph (314 km/h)
0-62 mph (100 km/h)	3.8 seconds	4 seconds
Weight	3,637 pounds (1,650 kg)	3,153 pounds (1,430 kg)
Estimated Base Price	$280,000	$170,000

According to Audi, more than 700 Audi designers and engineers helped the Lamborghini team create the Gallardo—about all the Lamborghini employees combined.

The Gallardo Spyder roof can raise or lower in about 20 seconds.

Lamborghini designed the Gallardo to be a high-performance car for everyday driving. Although Americans can't get the European rear video/TV option, they have snapped up the "everyday" car.

Charging Ahead

The modern Lamborghini factory in Sant'Agata Bolognese commands a sprawling view of former farmlands. The new owners have updated and added to the facility, including creating display areas for special cars and constructing the Lamborghini Museum. Audi leadership also revived Ferruccio Lamborghini's focus on customer service. It plans to open more dealerships and service centers worldwide.

Lamborghini, Ferrari, and Maserati—three famous sports car companies—operate factories in a ten-mile circle around Modeno, Italy.

BERTONE

For decades, European carmakers focused solely on frames and engines. They purchased body designs from other companies, such as Bertone in Italy. Today, Lamborghini has its own in-house design team.

Fast Fact

Bertone created several Lamborghini designs, such as the sleek Miura and wild Countach.

Miura Concept car

Lamborghini paid tribute to the 40th anniversary of the Miura with the unveiling of a special Miura Concept car at the 2006 North American International Automobile Show in Detroit. Lamborghini big-wigs say they won't ever produce the car. Never say never!

Luc Donckerwolke

A new car starts with designer drawings. Luc Donckerwolke, a Belgian designer, led the Lamborghini team on the Murciélago and Gallardo projects.

About 700 people work in the Lamborghini car factory today. They build more than 1,600 vehicles yearly—far less than the 250,000 vehicles just one Chevrolet plant could produce in a year.

Registro Lamborghini

Ferruccio Lamborghini recorded details on each car. His archives disappeared in the mid1990s. Now, *Registro Lamborghini* encourages owners to register their cars online and fill the data gaps.

Some experts guess that about 10,000 Lamborghinis exist today.

restoration
to return something to its former condition

In the past, Lamborghini built less than 300 cars in a year.

Many older Lamborghinis need serious fix-ups. The new Lamborghini **Restoration** Centre provides owners with factory details for true restoration.

Workers handcraft each Lamborghini car, one by one, just as they have done since 1963. One difference: computers help fine-tune the engines.

23

Honoring the Past

Automobili Lamborghini marked its 40th anniversary with a rich legacy for such a young car company. Today, two museums in Italy honor Ferruccio Lamborghini and his cars. Many Lamborghini cars have also crowned displays at art and car museums around the globe. Many sites on the Internet pay tribute to the House of the Fighting Bull.

Americans look forward to spotting a Lamborghini in the New York City Columbus Day Parade, honoring Italian-American heritage. Automobili Lamborghini has sent cars just for the event.

The official Lamborghini Museum is located at the headquarters in Sant'Agata.

In 1995, Ferruccio's son, Tonino, opened a museum to honor his father. It features classic Lamborghini cars and tractors—even a Lamborghini Helicopter prototype.

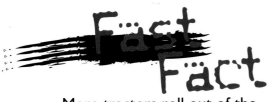

More tractors roll out of the Trattori factory in just one year than all the Lamborghini sports cars built since 1963.

In Europe, it's easier to spot a Lamborghini tractor than a Lamborghini car.

Revved to Race

Unlike many carmakers, Lamborghini didn't enter racing to advertise its cars. Ferruccio Lamborghini blocked a Formula One (F1) program because of the high costs. After Ferruccio retired, Lamborghini engineers developed a V-12 F1 engine to sell to racing teams. It never claimed a checkered flag. Lamborghini quit F1 at the end of the 1993 season. Now Lamborghini is revved up to race on its own terms.

Fast Fact

Lamborghini built only 50 Diablo SVRs in 1996, but it was enough to jump-start racing interest.

*Lamborghini designed the Diablo SVR mainly for the Lamborghini **Monomarque** Championship. Its five-speed V-12 could reach 186 miles (300 km) per hour. The race-ready 1999 Diablo GTR could hit 210 miles (338 km) per hour.*

In 2003, Lamborghini offered a race-ready Murciélago R-GT. It had rear-wheel drive to meet GT and **endurance**-racing rules. It took third place in its first race.

The base price for an original Murciélago R-GT was about $600,000.

endurance
power or strength to keep going or continue for a long time or distance

monomarque
in racing, cars of one brand or model

2006 Gallardo Race Package

Lamborghini offered the 2006 Gallardo with racing options, such as a racing steering wheel, steering, and suspension. It's mainly for club racing.

More Than Fast Cars

Back in 1968, Ferruccio Lamborghini modified his 400GT engine to hype his speed boat. Since then, Lamborghini's Motor Marini has built more than 400 marine engines. Several of these powerplants have sped to the finish line in Class 1 Offshore World Championship boats.

In 2001, Lamborghini's marine engine won the 2001 Offshore World Championship Time Trial.

Like all cars, Lamborghinis can be modified with **aftermarket** products. A few aftermarket products mimic Lamborghini. Pivoting door adaptors make ordinary car doors swing like the famous Countach.

aftermarket
parts added to a vehicle after its sale to the owner

Tonino Lamborghini built an unusual Lamborghini car: a neighborhood electric vehicle or NEV. Of course, it's beautiful and fast (for a golf car), topping 25 miles (40 km) per hour.

One of the best places to catch the Lamborghini spirit is through Lamborghini Club America. These Lamborghini car owners and wanna-be owners host several events during the year and publish a magazine. Expect the legendary Italian marque to push the driving experience to new extremes, as it has from the start.

Glossary

aerodynamics (ahr oh dih NAM iks) – engineering designs that allow air to flow easily over the body for greater speed

aftermarket (AFF tur MAR kit) – parts added to a vehicle after its sale to the owner

carburetors (KAR bah ray turz) – a device for mixing fuel with air for the engine to burn

chassis (CHASS ee) – the frame that supports the body of a vehicle

clutch (KLUCH) – a part of the engine's transmission used to shift gears

endurance (en DUR ahns) – power or strength to keep going or continue for a long time or distance

marque (MARK) – the logo for an automobile manufacturer or its models

monomarque (MAH no mark) – in racing, cars of one brand or model

restoration (reh STOR ah shun) – to return something to its former condition

Further Reading

Jolliffe, David with Willard, Tony. *Lamborghini: Forty Years*. Motorbooks International, 2004.

Phillips, Adam. *Supercars: Driving the Dream*. Barnes and Noble Books, 2006.

Pritchard, Anthony. *Lamborghini: Supercars from Sant'Agata*. Haynes Publications, 2005.

Websites

www.lamborghini.com

www.lambocars.com

www.lamborghiniusa.com

www.lamborghiniregistry.com

Index

About the Author

Tracy Nelson Maurer writes nonfiction and fiction books for children, including more than 50 titles for Rourke Publishing LLC. Tracy lives with her husband Mike and two children near Minneapolis, Minnesota.